Alessandra Migliaccio

The Mirror Game

The behavioral path of the motor activity

The Mirror Game – The behavioral path of the motor activity

ISBN: 9798843992705

Translation of the book "Lo specchio riflesso – La via comportamentale dell'attività motoria" by Alessandra Migliaccio, © 2022.

Graphic design: Vincenzo Maione alias Becho © 2022.
www.vincenzomaione.com

Alessandra Migliaccio

The Mirror Game

The behavioral path of the motor activity

A didactic proposal for pupils with autism spectrum disorder
for Italian primary school and first grade secondary school
(US "grade school")

Preface by Dr. Rosaria Benincasa

"The rules of imitation do not limit the autistic individual, but provide coordinates for living experiences in their simplicity".

Vincenzo Maione

Table of Contents

Foreword 1
Preface 3
Introduction 5
Chapter I 7
  Sport and inclusion 9
  Cycle of education 17
  Adaptations 24
  Motor game in a behavioral key 26
Chapter II 31
  Working hypotheses 33
  Strategy and operational method 38
  Preparation of the program 39
  Results 43
  Graphs 45
  Discussion and conclusion 49
Acknowledgements 51
References 55

List of Figures

Figure 1 - Firefighters in pairs - Position of the players 29
Figure 2 - Firefighters in pairs - The peteca on the cloth........ 30
Figure 3 - Graph "To stay at least 1 m away from the playmate" 46
Figure 4 - Graph "Rate of the data of the eye contact with the playmate" 47
Figure 5 - Graph "Imitation" 48

Foreword

This study[1], full of ideas and suggestions for sensitive and motivated educators, highlights the role and the function of the motor activity within the behavioral pathway, an elective strategy in the treatment of children with autism spectrum disorder. The purpose of the study is to demonstrate how motor activity, through individualized and ad hoc built procedures, can facilitate the integration and the socialization of a pupil with autism spectrum disorder. In particular, through the motor activity in the "Peteca" game, the duration of the social interaction, the joint attention, and the imitation can be increased, expanding the spontaneous communicative repertoire of requests (mand) and of answers to questions (intraverbal) as a correlated datum.

Keywords: autism, imitation, proxemics, eye contact, social behavior, peteca game.

[1] The title "The Mirror Game" refers to a game for children, which develops expressive skills and mastery of one's body. Its objective is the imitation of the movements of the playmate. Imitation is the pivotal area for learning and, in this case, it has been developed through the sport game of the Peteca.

Preface

By Dr. Rosaria Benincasa

Writing the preface of a book of Alessandra is an honor and a commitment for me. I observed the work of Alessandra with admiration, the progress of her knowledge on a so delicate subject, which blends with the Applied Behavior Analysis naturally and which broadens its boundaries above all. The love and the passion, which Alessandra has lavished in her work and which contains her wish to improve the quality of life of her students, are inferred from a careful examination of the text clearly. The inclusion of pupils with disabilities represents an essential assignment of our school system, because it embodies a shared social value really and applies a precise (Italian) constitutional regulation: the fundamental principle of equality (article 3). The knowledge of all themes linked with the integration of the services and the development of facilitating procedures represent an essential way of working. Improving the competence in inclusive teaching in all teachers becomes the decisive factor for the integration of the pupil with disabilities and, as a consequence, for his personal development as an individual. In the latest classification, the WHO refers to terms that analyze the health of a person in a positive key: functioning and health. The ICF (International Classification of Functioning, Disability and Health) wants to provide a broad analysis of the state of health of individuals by placing the correlation between health and environment, arriving at the definition of disability, meant as a health condition in an unfavorable environment. What matters is to intervene in the social environment by building networks of meaningful services that reduce disability. The main contribution of this work lies in having investigated the possibility of facilitating, through the use of methodological behavioral strategies of the Applied Behavior Analysis (ABA), the practice of sport for pupils with autism spectrum disorder, with the aim of supporting the school in finding valid strategies to avoid the discomfort of pupils, who encounter obstacles in the acquisition of one or more skills constantly, and remain on the fringe of the social life, not just the school one, consequently.

Introduction

The work as a support teacher, which I perform at the Comprehensive Institute "Salvatore Di Giacomo 3", S. Chiara, Qualiano, Naples, Italy, and that as a trainer for the Italian Paralympic Committee and at CONI for activities of adapted motor training, has led me to answer always equal questions, as time passed, about the possibility to allow all children with disabilities to practice motor activity at school effectively, but in particular those autistic pupils, who place the teacher in front of a rather complex methodological problem.

Being aware of all the real challenges that this type of disability entails, I have made the attempt to develop a gradual and realistic research path based on the behavioral analysis, in order to suggest a series of methodological strategies on motor games, after having checked them daily, on the specificity of the case, arriving at expanding the repertoire of the behaviors of the individual or at replacing the present maladaptive behaviors, thanks to the supervision of Dr. Rosaria Benincasa, psychologist, behavior analyst, Board Certified Behavior Analyst® (BCBA®)[2].

[2] The Board Certified Behavior Analyst® (BCBA®) is a postgraduate certification in behavior analysis. Certified professionals at BCBA® level are independent professionals, who provide services of behavioral analysis. The Behavior Analyst Certification Board (BACB®) is an American body established in 1998 to define standards and requirements of training, supervision and internship that are necessary to have the qualification of Certified Behavior Analyst.

The purpose is to extract useful and repeatable elements that can be applied to the school reality which, second only to family as a place of life, encounters the specific difficulties of the pupil in a direct and continuous way daily.

"*The Applied Behavior Analysis, (ABA), is used to support people with developmental delay in at least six ways*[3]*:*

1. *Increasing adaptive behaviors and skills;*
2. *Facilitating the learning of new skills and knowledge;*
3. *Maintaining socially acceptable adaptive behaviors;*
4. *Extending and generalizing behaviors and skills from one setting to another and from one situation to another;*
5. *Reducing the conditions where problem behaviors occur; and*
6. *Reducing the intensity and the frequency of problem behaviors*".

This study proposes the test and the verification through the analysis of the data collected on the manipulation of those independent variables, introduction of the peteca game, which can modify the behavior, a dependent variable, correlated to it.

This body was created to protect users of services of behavior analysis to ensure that the professionals had adequate training and experience. Credentials established by the Board: BCBA® (Board Certified Behavior Analyst®): the professional must have a full university degree and must have passed an ABA master's degree level II or similar courses. The BCBA® designs and supervises behavioral analytic interventions, oversees the work of the Board Certified Assistant Behavior Analysts (BCaBA®), and of the therapists who implement the interventions (RBT®).

[3] Moderato P., Copelli C., " *L'Analisi Comportamentale Applicata. Parte prima: teoria, metateoria, fondamenti*", page 32, Università UILM-IESCUM.

Chapter I

The Mirror Game

Sport and inclusion

During my experience in training courses for colleagues of motor education, the questions, which they always asked me, just concerned that they wanted to have the "*perfect recipe*" to teach also children suffering from autism spectrum syndrome. So, thanks to my work in this situation, at school, I tried to understand what was the most suitable methodology to create truly inclusive sports game opportunities, which could help the acquisition of adequate social behaviors on the one hand, and of a greater knowledge (I mean both for teachers and students) of one of their classmates, perhaps defined a little bizarre, rigid, and strange, up to that moment, on the other hand.

I can affirm that the methodology of the behavior analysis, if applied with scientific rigor, proves to be useful for the acquisition not only of more adequate social behaviors, but it also allows the admission and the active participation of these children in sports and recreational groups, PON and projects, not completely accessible up to this moment, because they have been structured in an ineffective way many times. The current research in behavioral analysis, applied to sports performance, has laid the foundations (I assume that further research will be needed), so that it can be used at all levels of sport and in all sports successfully, not only by neurotypical individuals, but for those suffering from autism spectrum disorder above all.

For my work, I availed myself of some scientific sources[4]. The majority of the examined research is divided into three currents mainly: that one with an analytic behavioral basis, that one of socio-cognitive origin, and of social origin finally. In particular, what scientific research investigates belongs to sports practice declined in three different areas.

The first contribution can be referred to the analytic behavioral current: "*A literature review: Applied Behavior Analysis and performance; the Past, the Present, and the Future*" by A. Molly Patrice Fields[5].

This and further papers are available on the website: https://bearworks.missouristate.edu/theses, Part of the Applied Behavior Analysis, Missouri State University, Recommended Citation-Fields, Molly Patrice, "*A Literature Review: Applied Behavior Analysis and Performance; the Past, the Present, and the Future*" (2020). MSU Graduate Theses. 3589. https://bearworks.missouristate.edu/theses/3589.

---

[4] Overview: Initial Publication Rushall, B. S., & Siedentop, D. (1972). The developmental and control of behavior in sport and physical education. Philadelphia, PA: Lea & Febiger. Recommended Reading Luiselli, J. K., & Reed, D. D. (Eds.). (2011). Behavioral sport psychology: Evidence-based approaches to performance enhancement. New York: Springer. Martin, G. L. (2019). Applied sport psychology: Practical guidelines from behavior analysis (6th ed). Winnipeg, Canada: Sport Science Press. Luiselli, J. K., Woods, K. E., & Reed, D. D. (2011). Review of sports performance research with youth, collegiate, and elite athletes. Journal of Applied Behavior Analysis, 44, 999-1002.

[5] A Master's Thesis Submitted to the Graduate College of Missouri State University in Partial Fulfillment of the Requirements for the Degree of Master of Science, Applied Behavior Analysis- Seniuk, H. A., Witts, B. N., Williams, W. L., Ghezzi, P. M. (2013). Behavioral coaching. The Behavior Analyst, 36, 167-72. Martin, G. L., Thompson, K., & Regehr, K. (2004). Studies using single-subject designs in sport psychology: 30 years of research. The Behavior Analyst, 27, 263-280.

The second is of a socio-cognitive origin[6] instead: (Albert Bandura), "*Aspetti psicosociali dello Sport per la Disabilità Giovanile*" Jeffrey J. Martin, 2006. "*Psychosocial aspects of youth disability sport*", Adapted Physical Activity Quarterly, 23 (1), 65-77, available at the website of the Wayne State University: http://digitalcommons.wayne.edu/coe_khs/17.

The third deals with "*A Meta-Analytic Review of the Efficacy of Physical Exercise Interventions on Cognition in Individuals with Autism Spectrum Disorder and ADHD*", by Beron W. Z. Tan, Julie A. Pooley and Craig P. Speelman, published online July 13 2016. The article is available on the Springerlink.com website. Keywords: Meta-analysis, exercise intervention, ADHD cognition, Autism.

With the first contribution, the research area is certainly behavioral. The majority of the skills and of the techniques in sport can be divided also into behaviors[7], which are often objectives within the game, such as, for instance, final goals, scoring points, scoring home runs, scoring touchdowns, etc. Behaviors exist in the realm of sport within the participation in

---

[6] The social cognitive theory of A. Bandura (1986, 1997). Albert Bandura, a developmental psychologist, is famous for his theory of social learning, according to which children learn in a social environment by imitating the behavior of others, and for the concept of self-efficacy, with which he refers to the belief of being able to be successful. or to fail in a performance.

[7] By J. M. Johnston H. S. Pennypacker; James M. Johnston; Taylor & Francis Inc, 1993 "Readings for Strategies and Tactics of Behavioral Research", (Johnston and Pennypacker, 1993, p. 23) Technical definition: the human behavior includes everything that a person does, how moves and what says, thinks and feels. "*It is the interaction of the organism with the environment, which is characterized by a detectable movement, in space and in time, of some parts of the organism and which results in a measurable change in at least one aspect of the environment*".

sport itself, on the bench, in coaching decisions, and from the public also. Behavioral analysis, applied to sport, could have many different shapes and dimensions. It could be used, and has been used in past research, to reduce unwanted behaviors during the sports performance, to increase technically valid skills within the performance (which can help to reduce the chances of lesions or to increase the productivity and the accuracy of the performance), or to increase the quality of a "mental game" of the athlete, which could include the awareness and/or the definition of the objectives. Research in applied behavioral analysis and in sports performance has laid the foundations for it to be used in all levels of sport successfully.

In the second contribution, the author investigated the psychosocial aspects of participation in sport with children suffering from disabilities, which were examined using the socio-cognitive theory and the model of sports commitment. "Therefore, understanding the involvement of children with disabilities in sport from a psychosocial perspective is the primary aim of the current study". ("*Aspetti psicosociali dello Sport per la Disabilità Giovanile*", Jeffrey J. Martin).

The guiding theory for the current study derives from the social cognitive theory (Bandura, 1997) and from sport as a model of engagement (Scanlan, Carpenter, Simons, Schmidt and Keeler, 1993a). Numerous scientists have examined important psychological and social aspects of the involvement of children and of youth in sport and in physical activity (Brustad, 1992; Weiss & Smith, 1999; Weiss & Stuntz, 2004), therefore, the increase in physical activity, such as that obtained through participation in sport, can affect the quality of the life correlated with health positively (Rejeski, Brawley & Shumaker, 1996). Moreover, people with disabilities often have less extended social networks and less friends than non-disabled people (McNeil, 1993), this makes the sports environment a potentially attractive social opportunity for children, who want stronger relationships with children of the same age. To be with friends, taking part in sport, is a primary reason for youth sport (Weiss & Ferrer-Caja, 2002).

The third contribution, "*A Meta-Analytic Review of the Efficacy of Physical Exercise Interventions on Cognition in Individuals with Autism Spectrum Disorder and ADHD*", is a meta-analytic review of the effectiveness of physical exercise and of the interventions on cognition in individuals with autism spectrum disorder and ADHD.

For the inclusion in this meta-analysis, participants in the study had to have been diagnosed with ADHD[8] or ASD[9], including disorders that were previously known as autism, Asperger's, and pervasive developmental disorders not otherwise specified (American Psychiatric Association, 2013). This research attempts to study the efficacy of the intervention of the physical exercise on cognition in both disorders, simultaneously and separately in terms of executive dysfunction, (EF), of some specific physical exercises. Domains are generally reported as compromised in individuals with ASD and ADHD,

---

[8] ADHD stands for Attention Deficit Hyperactivity Disorder. It is about a neurodevelopmental disorder characterized by well-defined and continuous symptoms, such as: difficulty in paying attention and maintaining concentration; impulsive behaviors; and physical restlessness. Some areas of the daily life, such as school and friendships, are significantly affected by this disorder, which torments about 2% of children, especially boys, in Italy.

[9] ASD: Autism Spectrum Disorders are a heterogeneous set of neurodevelopmental disorders, characterized by a persistent deficit in social communication and in social interaction in multiple contexts and patterns of behaviors, restricted and repetitive interests or activities.

if compared with healthy individuals separately, these relate to aspects of planning (e.g., Chen et al. 2016; Hill 2004), set-shifting[10] and memory of work (e.g.: Chen et al. 2016; Andersen et al. 2015), sustained attention and even inhibition. The studies have used the exercise as an intervention tool in the evaluation of some aspects of the cognitive objective performance. The benefits of the physical exercise have been widely recognized both in literature (e.g., McMorris et al. 2009) and by media (Leavy et al. 2011; Marcus et al. 1998). Its reported positive effects can be broadly classified into physical health (for example WHO[11], 2010), behavioral (for instance Sowa and Meulenbroek, 2012), cognitive (for example Kramer and Erickson, 2007), and health or psychosocial functioning (for instance Netz et al., 2005). The results reveal a small to medium overall effect of the exercise on cognition and assert the effectiveness of exercise interventions, to improve some aspects of cognitive performance in individuals with ASD and/or ADHD. Moreover, thanks to the exercise, mainly positive effects emerged on cognitive performance, above all on that of the executive functions (EF) (for example Kramer and Erickson, 2007, and Tomporowski et al., 2008). The studies of Sibley and Etnier (2003) reported that the effect of exercise does not depend on the kind of physical exercises, but meta-analyses of Fedewa and Ahn (2011) have found a greater positive effect of the aerobic exercise than other types of interventions of exercise (e.g., perceptive-motor exercises). Moreover, other meta-analyses have found a greater post-exercise cognitive capacity in the youngest children (Sibley and Etnier 2003; Fedewa and Ahn 2011). Furthermore, the effect of the exercise is selective and affects some areas of cognition more than others. This will

[10] Set-shifting refers to the ability to change attention focus/objective following different stimuli/conditions.

[11] World Health Organization.

facilitate the progress in the science of the use of exercise to improve cognition, identifying which areas of cognition are not affected by physical exercise and which factors limit its effectiveness (e.g., level of physical constitution, and diagnosis).

The fourth and last contribution, still of a behavioral origin, is: "*The influence of child-preferred activities on autistic children's social behavior*" by Robert L. Koegel, University of California, Santa Barbara, Kathleen Dyer, The May Institute, Lynn K. Bell, University of California, Santa Barbara, published in the Journal of Applied behavior analysis, Number 3 (FAU1987). Descriptors: social behavior, response to avoidance, autism, preferred activities, clinical research.

"*One of the characteristics of the autistic children is a serious behavior of social avoidance*" (Hops, 1983; Kanner, 1943; Schreibman, Koegel, Charlop, and Egel, 1982). The research assesses if the kind of activities, to which the children were exposed, the preferred ones, compared to activities that were determined by an adult arbitrarily, was correlated with the quantity of avoidance behaviors expressed. The results revealed a negative correlation between the activities preferred by the children and the behaviors of social avoidance. Further analyses revealed that:

a) Behaviors of social avoidance could be manipulated within a design of inversion and would decrease, predictably, when the children were encouraged to start appropriate preferred activities; and
b) These procedures could be used to teach the children to start preferred activities in public environments, with consequent reductions in the responses of social avoidance, also after the suggestions of the therapist have been completely removed.

The mentioned researches are some examples of studies on the results achieved about the effects of exercise and of sport in children and adolescents with developmental disabilities, to date. Although a connection emerges between the learning difficulties and the social skills, few systematic syntheses are available, which deal with the efficacy of sport (in relation with other special interventions for children with learning disorders) associated with a reduction of the maladaptive behavior in children with disabilities, and also with a better physical constitution, self-esteem, and social competence.

Cycle of education

The motor activity for children with autism spectrum[12] disorder, although is encouraged, places the teacher in front of a series of difficulties in its implementation, due to the nature, which characterizes this disorder and which involves a series of mainly methodological reflections.

First of all, the motor behavior is a social behavior, which develops and remains in the context thanks to mechanisms of natural reinforcement, such as interaction with others, the pleasure experienced in doing together and, helping the perception of the other person, teaches to understand his intentions and to act accordingly. Interaction is the way by which language is acquired and the reason why it is maintained, but, for children with autism spectrum disorder, this social motivation is not so automatic, because they do not find obtaining and interaction with other people as reinforcing and, therefore, the proposed stimuli just do not work.

Although pupils with autism spectrum disorder are generally able-bodied, they do not learn from the environment often, and the social deficit in childhood reduces the participation in the

[12] Taken from slides of the course by Dr. Rosaria Benincasa, Board Certified Behavior Analyst, BCBA®, "ABA e insegnamento delle abilità accademiche", Strategie di insegnamento dal curriculum base a quello intermedio, corso Sophis Academy 2018-Autismo; *Neurodiversity, meant as a developmental condition that is qualitatively different from typical development. In this perspective, there are no problems to be solved, but particular characteristics, in front of which it is necessary to adapt the working environment, our behavior, and the ways of intervention.*

learning experiences. This represents a primary objective of intervention and imposes that the educating community must rethink training and professional updating, because the traditional methodologies, which are normally effective for teaching a class group, fail with autistic pupils inexorably.

The inability to engage in these behaviors creates a strong obstacle to learning and to the development of sociability. Therefore, it becomes impossible to respond adequately to a child, who neither sends nor receives signals in the way that we are naturally equipped to receive or to send them. Hence the need to rethink the teaching methodology, asking ourselves about possible problematic behaviors, which could prevent both the child from learning new skills, and others from being effective in the organization of proposals. "*The diagnosis of autism in itself does not give specific indications on the educational needs and on the learning style: children are different from one another, we have to adapt the work environment, our behavior and the methods of intervention to the characteristics and to the individual needs by selecting objectives and strategies of teaching*"[13].

Before proposing any motor game, it would be essential to have a clear picture of the skills mastered by the pupil, to know well the level of his achieved development, his possessed and emerging skills, that is, those behaviors which need little help, in order to be implemented effectively.

---

[13]Taken from slides of the course by Dr. Rosaria Benincasa, BCBA® (Board Certified Behavior Analyst®) "ABA e insegnamento delle abilità accademiche", Strategie di insegnamento dal curriculum base a quello intermedio, corso Sophis Academy 2018.

To assess the developmental state of the child correctly, it would be useful to know how to use the VB-MAPP "Assessment of the fundamental developmental stages of the verbal behavior and planning of interventions"[14]. The handbook provides directions for planning each of the 170 Milestones (learning milestones), together with suggestions for the objectives of the IEP[15], and represents a good starting point for evaluating the repertoire of the existing skills, to structure a program later on, which is based on the results obtained. Translated into the school environment, it means "to select the objectives on the basis of the level and of the functionality of the child, bearing in mind that for the motor activity it is necessary at least an intermediate level 2 VB MAPP curriculum with imitative skill".

Once the data have been collected, we proceed in a work of integration between the skills that we want to teach and those owned by the pupil. Without this intermediate step, we risk proposing high-effort activities or, vice versa, low-effort activities, which will not allow us to achieve the expected objective.

---

[14] Mark L. Sundberg, Ph.D. VB MAPP, "*Assessment delle tappe evolutive fondamentali del comportamento verbale e programmazione degli interventi*", Vannini Editoria scientifica.

[15] The Individualized Educational Plan (IEP) is the pedagogical device on which the scholastic inclusion of pupils with disabilities is based. It must define an educational and didactic pathway that calls teachers, families and extra school actors to share responsibility.
The Italian Legislative Decree 66/2017 on school inclusion offers an opportunity to rethink the IEP in the light of the biopsychosocial perspective introduced by the International Classification of the Functioning of Disability and Health (ICF), according to the provisions of the Italian Interministerial Decree 182/2020.

Therefore, the experimental analysis of a motor behavior, which we want to be learned, starts from the relation that exists between the events of the environment (stimuli), in this case gymnasium, small gymnastic apparatus, music, if it is provided, whistle, and the behavior of the organism (the answers can be the most different and can range from avoidance/escape to the increase of stereotypy, isolation, echolalias, etc., and lack of reciprocation) in the attempt to demonstrate that, manipulating some of them, others change. The organization of the gymnasium environment, meant as an independent variable (that is, it exists in itself as an already structured and coded environment), can "elicit", that is, evoke, the observable response of the organism (dependent variable, that is, the behavior derives from and depends on the stimuli, to which it has been exposed previously). If we want the pupil to learn a motor game, in the task-analysis of the motor task, we must organize all the contingency relationships among the behavior, the events that precede it with a discriminative function (that is, salient with respect to the context and that indicate to the pupil the possibility to act), and the events that follow it with a reinforcing function (the teacher or the classmates, who praise him, the access to his "reinforcer" (Premack's principle) or to a counter of the token[16] (symbolic reinforcer)), but also to specify the cost of the response[17].

---

[16] The token economy is a system of behavioral change consisting of three main components:

a) A specific list of target behaviors;
b) Tokens or scores, which participants receive for issuing the target behaviors, and
c) A list of reinforcing items of exchange items, preferred activities or privileges that the participants obtain by exchanging the tokens that they have earned.

[17] The cost of the response is the term used to remove a reinforcement for an unwanted behavior.

During the teaching/learning process, we must think about organizing our work, starting from those motor behaviors already acquired by the child, continuing towards what Vygotskij (1934) defined the zone of proximal development, that is, "*the distance between the real level of development, as it is determined by autonomous problem solving, and the level of potential development, as it is determined through problem solving under the guidance of an adult or in collaboration with the most capable peers*"[18].

"*The first question to ask ourselves is: what could be the difficulties of a social environment, whose communication contents are high if compared to the possessed skills? Placing a child in a class, whose contents of the daily verbal communication are above his level of understanding, represents one of the problems that are most significantly related to an effective social inclusion. [...] such inclusion must be also useful and offer the child social models of interaction with children of the same age". Usually, in the school environment, in team work, the pupils respond to a complex language with an intermittent reinforcement, (let us think about making a score, in a team game, it does not mean that the pupils win the game immediately, but a certain period of time will pass before the game ends) the attention is continuous, the teacher moves in a wide space, often without reference points, and all this for an autistic child is difficult to decode, above all if he lacks the basic prerequisites, such as:*

- *Functional use of the objects, stereotypies must not rouse;*

[18] Ricci C., Romeo A., Bellifemmine D., Corradori G., Magaudda C. (2014), "*Il Manuale ABA -VB Applied Behavior Analysis and Verbal Behavior" 2017. Chapter 4, page 77-* Erickson.

- *Imitation: divided into group imitation and imitations of game actions;*
- *Anticipation, that is, monitoring the glance;*
- *Response to the signal, for example "Ready! Steady! Go!" or "At my three you will go"; and*
- *Imitation of the adult or of the playmate as a choral response.*

In this case we work on parallel skills, that is, those skills that can be maintained in a group, creating an increase in the competence of the child in understanding instructions and answer to questions on education, on the imitation of the response (where it is lacking or even absent, otherwise the child will have problems playing with others), in the joint attention, through structured material, and fading the aids or prompts."[19]
(*Ref. Dr. Rosaria Benincasa, Board Certified Behavior Analyst, BCBA®, from the course "Le abilità accademiche di base"*).

Therefore, since we want that our pupils play with the others and that they implement socially adequate behaviors, it is important to understand the contingencies, which govern the stimuli-behavior-consequences relation, and to control all those conditions, which underlie the interactions. between the individual and the environment.

Effectiveness and quickness of learning depend on the teaching procedures used to achieve the formulated objectives.

---

[19] Taken from the online course provided by Dr. Rosaria Benincasa BCBA® (Board Certified Behavior Analyst®) "*Abilità accademiche dal curricolo di base a quello intermedio*" organized by the Accademia Sophis -2018.

The indispensable conditions to an effective teaching are:

1. Control of the stimuli, that is, environmental structuring;
2. Organization of materials; and
3. Control over education.

Adaptations

The purpose of the present work is to provide some operational strategies, which could be a basis for reflection to make conscious methodological choices, because they are based on a scientific methodology.

"*The illustration of these operational paths can allow a further methodological deepening and a reflection on one's daily work. Anyone, who is engaged in professions that involve the interaction of single individuals, can notice that some precise measures are needed to transform the experiences developed in educational or rehabilitative contexts into applied research, the results of which, lending themselves to intersubjective evaluation, can enrich the operational knowledge in particular sectors (...) such as the sports area".*

"The story of the individual with atypical development includes conditions and events that inhibit the opportunities for learning and for acquiring new skills and new forms of behavior in different degrees. These considerations involve study, implementation and verification of environmental solutions aimed to expand the behavioral repertoire of the individual by making him learn more and more complex and appropriate behaviors"[20].

Both from an ethical and from a pragmatic point of view, any behavior, set as a goal for change, must benefit the person

[20] Giovanni Maria Guazzo, "*L'Analisi Comportamentale Applicata*" Strategie educative per genitori e insegnanti, IRFID (Istituto per la Ricerca, la Formazione e l'Informazione sulle Disabilità), 2011, page 25.

directly or indirectly, that is, we should help to clarify the social significance related to the habilitating value.

Howhins (1984) suggested that "*the potential significance of any behavioral change should be judged in the context of habilitation*", which he defined as follows: "Habilitation (adaptation) is the degree where the repertoire of the person maximizes short and long term reinforcers for that individual and for the others, and minimizes short and long term punishers. In this case, the skills taught could be used in the game with the peers in the future, both in the class group and outside it, and this could lead the pupils to have more social interactions that are typical of their age and to be accepted by the group of the peers.

Consequently, participation and access to extra-curricular sports projects could increase, thus ensuring the maintenance of learned skills, providing opportunities for learning other adaptive behaviors at the same time, to arrive to the maximum inclusion in the ordinary society to which they belong, at the end, according to the principle of normalization."[21], quoted in the book Applied Behavior Analysis.

---

[21] J.O. Cooper, T.E. Heron, W. L. Hevard, "*Applied Behavior Analysis*", Italian version, ABC Centro ABA. Quot. page 173: "The principle of normalization refers to the use of more typical environments, expectations and procedures progressively "to establish and/or to maintain personal behaviors that are as culturally normal as possible" (Wolfensberger, 1972, page 28)". Normalization is not a single technique, but a philosophical position, which aims to achieve the maximum physical and social integration of people with disabilities in the ordinary society. In addition to the philosophical and ethical reasons, to select the appropriate target behaviors for age and for setting, it is necessary to repeat that the adaptive, independent and social behaviors, which come into contact with reinforcement, are more likely to be maintained than behaviors that do not do it.

Motor game in a behavioral key

The choice of the best sports activity, where to insert the pupil with autism spectrum disorder[22], has been complex, because it has been based on a delicate combination among the characteristics of the disorder, the individual peculiarities, the typical aspects of sports activity, and the organizational needs of the school environment.

The rules that I followed were the following:

1) The game can be performed in a small group and then generalized to the class;
2) The pupil knows and maintains his own spaces;
3) There is only one simple and clear rule;
4) The area of the game is well circumscribed, but little structured;
5) The patterns of the game are fixed and are not modified continuously based on the agreement between players;
6) The pupil can implement the expected behavior quickly;
7) The stimulated ability can affect other behaviors to a greater extent later on; and
8) The game is appropriate for the age of the pupil and allows a more rewarding exchange with the class environment to which he belongs.

---

[22] The term autism derives from the Greek "*autus*" and means "himself". Subtypes of autism: Asperger's, Heller's Syndrome, Rett's Syndrome, and Pervasive Developmental Disorder. DSM5 replaces the term autism with Autism Spectrum Disorder (ASD), and defines autism in terms of: "*Continuum of conditions, that is, different clinical frameworks with many characteristics in common, whose boundaries are faded*".

The proposal follows those ones regulated by CONI[23], but then it provides, for its effective learning, the deepening of the methodology and adapted technique according to the principles of the ABA (Applied Behavior Analysis).

Thus, in environments structured for the learning occurrence, a strategy is developed gradually, which leads to the achievement of, albeit modest, levels of autonomy, interaction, and communication.

In doing this, we should not neglect the group of pupils of the same age, who are precious resources of the educational process, and who come into contact with the pupil in a highly collaborative setting daily. Specifically, the inclusive game of the "*Peteca*" and of its variations was chosen. The choice fell on this game/motor activity, because it develops both the basic motor pattern of throwing, and the coordination skills of predicting trajectories, distances, rhythm of executive throwing and temporal sequences of the motor actions, and leads the pupil to organize his own movement in space in relation to himself, to the objects and to the others. Another fundamental aspect is the opportunity for the pupil to imitate the behavior of his classmates, to increase the attention span[24], to focus on the task, and to experience the "*joint control*" attention.

---

[23] Seclì P., Locatelli E., Milani M., Cazzoli S., (2017), "*Quaderni di Sport di classe –guida per tutor e docenti della scuola primaria*", CONI servizi SPA, Editore Calzetti & Mariucci.

[24] The attention span is the amount of time in which a person can stay focused and not get distracted, maintained attention. The element of inattention occurs when the individual is taken by other activities or sensations in an uncontrollable way. The ability to keep the attention on a task is crucial for achieving one's own objectives.

The first activity identified, as a prerequisite of the proposed game, was throwing, then the following games were proposed subsequently.

- **Firefighters in pairs**[25]
  The pupils arrange themselves in pairs, facing each other, on the short sides of a tablecloth, which is stretched out between them, and which they hold at the margins of the edges. A Peteca is placed in the center. At a signal, they throw the little ball, using the tablecloth that goes up, and retrieve the little ball, trying not to let it fall outside the tablecloth. The rhythm of the game is up/down.
- **Variation with two Petecas**
  A throwing competition, as in the previous activity, with two Petecas.
- **Variation with exchange of Petecas**
  At the signal, the teams of the pupils throw the Peteca, trying to make it fall into the cloth of the opponents.

[25] I *Quaderni Di Sport Di Classe* © 2020, Sport e Salute S.p.A.

Figure 1 - Firefighters in pairs - Position of the players

Figure 2 - Firefighters in pairs - The peteca on the cloth

Chapter II

Working hypotheses

Generalized developmental disorders constitute a spectrum of cognitive and behavioral disorders, characterized by a severe and generalized impairment in different areas of development: deficit of socialization, of verbal and non-verbal communication, of imaginative activity, and presence of restricted and repetitive manners of behavior. The deficits in imitation have been hypothesized as underlying the social, communication and affection disorders, and the deficit in the symbolic game and in the theory of the mind. Some authors assert that the system of the mirror neurons plays an important role in the development and in the expression of imitation, and that the symptoms associated with autism are ascribable to a dysfunction of this system. Given the early onset of the disorder, the study of the social and communication skills is of particular interest. These abilities develop in the first years of life, and, in particular, the precursors of the imitative behaviors, such as joint attention skills, eye contact, proxemics, and exchange of turns, being insufficient, play a primary role in the development of the communication and social difficulties that are characteristic of the autistic disorder. It is a well-established fact that the social deficit and the motor imitation deficit reduce the participation in the learning experiences. It remains to be clarified how to build this behavioral repertoire through the interaction with other people, when such interactions are not naturally reinforcing. These difficulties in imitating originate from the lack of motivation to do it[26].

---

[26] Chevallier C., Kohls G., Troiani V., Brodkin E. S. & Schultz R. T. (2012). "*The social motivation theory of autism. Trends in cognitive sciences*", 16(4), 231-239. The idea underlying the theory of the social

Therefore, imitation is a pivotal skill (ref. Dr. Rosaria Benincasa, BCBA®) in the future social cognitive and linguistic development.

Motor imitation is not a unitary ability in autism and, in the proposed approach, the target behavior has been identified in the duration of the social interaction which, expressed in behavioral terms, has taken into consideration three behaviors of the same subject:

- Proxemics, that is, to stay at least one meter away from the playmate;
- Eye contact; and
- Imitation of game actions with the playmate.

The strategy used to facilitate the social interaction has been the introduction of the Peteca game in pairs[27], which was performed by the subject in pairs with a classmate. The hypothesis under study has been to demonstrate how motor activity, through individualized and ad hoc built procedures, could facilitate integration and socialization of pupils with autism spectrum disorder, evaluated through the most used tools, based on the behavioral science (ABA), such as VB-MAPP of Sundberg[28] 2008 translated into Italian in 2012 and the "ABLL-

---

motivation is that the reward value of the social interactions, perceived as the pleasure deriving from them, feeds the interest in other people and promotes the participation in social experiences from early childhood. (Chevallier et al., 2012).

[27] Quaderni di sport di classe "*Guida didattica per tutor e docenti della scuola primaria*", vol. 2, 2018, Coni servizi S.p.A., Editore Calzetti & Mariucci.

[28] Sundberg, Ph.dM.l., "*Assessment delle tappe evolutive e fondamentali del comportamento verbale e programmazione degli interventi*", 2012, Vannini Editoria scientifica s.r.l. 1 VB-MAPP.

The Verbal Behavior Milestones Assessment and Placement Program (VB-MAPP – The assessment of the fundamental evolutionary stages of the verbal

S". In particular, through the motor activity in the "Peteca" game adapted to a pupil with intellectual disability and autism (for example with a score obtained through an intraverbal test[29] of 69.7, reference age 5 years), it is possible to increase: imitation, eye contact, proxemics, meant as staying at least one meter away from the playmate, increasing the communicative repertoire, as a by-product of the treatment.

The numerous studies published in this regard show a wide variability of results. The imitative performances in the many declinations seem to vary according to the type of movement requested (manual actions with objects, movements of the body, and oral-facial movements) and according to the nature of the task (functional imitation with objects, movements with parts of the body, with the whole body, up to sequences of more complex actions), and create a reciprocity, which represents a communicative bridge with the other person.

On the contrary, the student with a basic curriculum will not reciprocate the motor action, because he does not imitate, that is, he will not have joint attention on the object. Maybe he will not look at his playmate, who is passing him the ball (for example, but it can be any kind of object), and perhaps he will not have

---

behavior and planning interventions) is based on the Verbal Behavior of B. F. Skinner (1957), a reference point in the study of the language. The innovative work of Skinner, relative to the behavioral psychology and to learning, in addition to the study of the language, has led to the development of the applied behavior analysis (Applied Behavior Analysis - ABA). The VB-MAPP combines the procedures and the teaching methodology of the ABA with the analysis of the verbal behavior of Skinner. Its aim is to provide an instrument to evaluate the language, which is based on the behavioral principles, for all children with delays in language or other developmental disabilities.

[29] Sundberg and Sundberg, "*Intraverbal behavior and verbal conditional discriminations in typically developing children and children with autism*".

sequenced that the motor action is directed towards an aim, because he does not have the causal nexuses. Therefore, in a motor game, the pupil will have difficulty in perceiving the purposes of the game, in representing all those actions to himself mentally that, being connected together, lead to the achievement of the objective, in integrating the rules of the game together, and in implementing a successful anticipatory strategy, probably.

For this reason, an effective planning for the acquisition of the game will have the expression of the imitative repertoire as its objective. By opening this area, many other academic skills will be structured.

Numerous authors have suggested guidelines and criteria for the selection of target behaviors, which all turn around the question: "Whitin what limit will the proposed behavior change the life experience of the person?". An important preliminary step is to choose the behaviors, to be proposed as an objective, for an accurate and reliable measurement.

Behaviors can be described broadly as anything living beings do. The behaviors could be inherent to physical activity, to speaking, and to singing. Johnston and Pennypacker (1993) formulated a complete definition of behavior: "*The behavior of an organism is that part of the interaction of an organism with its environment, which is characterized by a detectable displacement in space through time of a part of the organism, and which translates into a measurable change in at least one aspect of the environment*"[30].

---

[30] James M. Johnston, Herry S. Pennypacker, "*Strategies and Tactics of Behavioral Research*", Green Gina, published by Routledge, 2008.

The writer starts from the hypothesis that an optimum model of sports activity could be developed for subjects with atypical development, if a serious procedural order is respected, since ***like all behaviors, so the motor one is observable, measurable, describable, endowed with frequency, intensity and duration, and underlies the laws of learning; and, as such, it can be modified***.

Above all, the research is aimed at those teachers, who find themselves dealing with the problem of asking performances that are adequate to the possibilities of their pupils daily, taking into account that motor behavior is not a field of activity, which involves only leisure, but is the fundamental tool to develop the first social skills and intersubjectivity, which result to be compromised in these subjects.

Strategy and operational method

An educational intervention was performed in the gym, involving a small group of the classmates of the pupil, in order to improve the social interaction in its behavioral components, such as eye contact, imitation of the game, and staying one meter away from the playmate.

The methodology, which has been used, was *modeling* and *shadowing* with *prompt* (help) from major to minor (*fading* or reduction of assistance). The introduction of the new activity has been signaled by a discriminative stimulus, that is, a symbol card, which enriched those ones that were present in his visual agenda of daily activities, and signaled by a stopwatch set for 40 minutes, which marked its start and its end.

With this strategy, the pupil showed himself:

- Favorable to the change of activity;
- Available for the change of classroom towards the gym;
- Available for learning, above all because the activity to be carried out is communicated to him in advance and, therefore, no behavioral rigidities are issued; and
- He has experienced the possibility to choose whom to play with.

The proposed material, that is, cloth, little balls, petecas, and placements, favored the participation in the proposed activities, in a place without sound distractors, because it was for the exclusive use of the small group.

Preparation of the program

Under the supervision of Dr. Rosaria Benincasa, Board Certified Behavior Analyst (BCBA®), the following objectives have been identified:

1. Baseline for the established objectives, data collection, and measurement (Phase A);
2. Treatment that the subject will perform with three playmates in the gym (Phase B); and
3. Behavioral analysis after the exposure to the treatment with data collection on permanent product (Phase AB) - *follow-up*, where to assess the stability of the desired behavioral changes after the end of the program.

- **Phase A**

As required by the experimental methodology, the basic measurement continued for different periods in the various school environments and has been focused on three objectives: staying at least one meter away from the playmate, imitation of the game with the playmate, and eye contact. They were also evaluated other aspects, connected to the program and linked to the possession of motor prerequisites useful for the success of the program. In this sense, with regard to the motor function, a checklist has been adopted for the collection of information, that is, a scale of evaluation elaborated by the writer, to ascertain and to define the skills mastered, the emerging ones and the lacking ones, in a specific way. It has been divided into areas, within which easily recordable small activities are planned. The set of the items contained in the evaluation form were very simple, some were only visible, while others required the execution of specific tests. The evaluation referred only to the absence (X) or to the presence (Y) of the degree of mastery of the pupil of basic skills, and of rhythmic and coordination skills.

The motor repertoire considered in emergency for the pupil concerned the following skills:

- To grasp the ball with both the arms stretched and then with a single hand for at least 3 meters;
- To throw a ball, with the arm moving both from the bottom upwards, for at least 2 meters, and from the top downwards for at least 2 meters;
- To throw and to intercept, recognizing and evaluating parabolas, trajectories, and distances; and
- Ability to imitate simple motor models.

The data collected:

- Provide a detailed picture of the starting situation and give way to understand which game and with which objectives will be priority as target behaviors in the proposed activities;
- Direct the attention of the observer to specific areas of the behavior; and
- Facilitate an objective verification of the situation of the pupil as time passes.

- **Phase B**

Training phase, the subject together with three playmates has been involved in a series of motor game activities, aimed at learning the Peteca motor game, with the construction of an imitative repertoire through *modeling* and the total physical guidance. The intervention focused on learning how to respond to clear instructions, which did not give rise to confusion. The verbal invitation has been always the same, in the event of no response, *prompts* have been provided on the answer, the child has been asked to repeat what was asked, then the progressive *fading* of the *prompt* has been made.

- **Follow up**

In this phase, as the experimental design prescribes, the treatment has been interrupted, while the monitoring of the skills of recalling of the pupil involved in the intervention has been continued. The used experimental design (A-B) required, as a preliminary datum of measurement, the analysis of the permanent product, that is, video recording the behavior, which can be measured in real time by observing the actions of a person, and recording the responses of interest, frequency (or *rate*), duration, and thus the effects on the environment as they occur. The measurement of the permanent products is an *ex post* method of data collection and concerns a change in the environment produced by a behavior, which lasts long enough to allow the measurement. The measurement of the permanent product does not refer to any specific method of measurement, instead it refers to a time (after that the behavior occurred) and to a means, that is, the effect of the behavior with which the measurer comes into contact, that is, observes the behavior.

Other aspects related to the program were assessed too, for example:

- To generalize and to maintain the behavior in the repertoire of the person in contexts and situations that are different from the initial one;
- To improve the social competence (to interact with other people in an equal way), for example to work with pupils never seen before;

- To improve the behavioral competence, such as to execute the instruction, to accept a physical contact, and to maintain the joint attention;
- To improve the fine eye-manual coordination;
- To increase the opportunities for learning, which the subject produces autonomously (reinforcement of the spontaneous behaviors towards the pursuit of adequate objectives, to understand a new game, adapting himself to new requests, and to imitate the classmates); and
- To stimulate the production of requests (*mand*) and answers to spontaneous questions (intraverbal) in the pupil, not directly related to the Peteca game, which could occur in places and times different from those ones prescribed for the treatment.

Results

The reference case concerned an experimental treatment, where a design of the A-B type was adopted on three behaviors of the pupil, to verify the effectiveness of the "Peteca motor game" strategy. The experimentation began in the years 2019/2020 and lasted throughout the year 2021.

Actually, with this experimental design, the same type of intervention is applied at different times for the different behaviors, which we have decided to modify. If this sequential introduction of the experimental variable determines an improvement in the assumed sense in all situations, this constitutes a strong proof of the effectiveness of the implemented intervention.

I assumed that the independent variable, peteca game, was useful for promoting the social inclusion of the pupil during the hour of motor activity executed with the belonging class group. The application of the experimental design has been on the same behavior, manifested by the same subject in different environments: small room for strengthening and gym.

The writer performed at least 3 basic measurements for each behavior, except for imitation because, after a first measurement, it was decided to intervene with a specific training for learning without errors.

The first phase corresponds to a moment of basic observation of the aspects, on which I shall have to intervene. This initial phase is followed by a phase of application of the variable of the treatment and by a final phase of interruption of the treatment, which took place during the summer months, and of evaluation on the effects of the treatment returning to school.

In the follow-up, the intervention was interrupted and, after returning to school, I checked the maintenance of the acquisitions as time passed. It should be noted that there has been the total maintenance of significant learning. The hypothesis, which the increase in interest in a new motor game developed with the playmate in a game context could cause an improvement in the relational field, has been shown by the growing trend of the social behaviors of the pupil, which happened to stabilize quite quickly. The visual analysis of the data demonstrates how it is possible to promote simple forms of social interaction through the peteca motor game for a person with disabilities of the autism spectrum, and how these acquisitions tend to be maintained and generalized.

Finally, a correlation was noted between the intervention and the increase in the verbal behavior, in the forms of *mand* (requests) and intraverbal (answers to questions), in the interaction with the classmates, which had a training of specific teaching later.

Graphs

Visual Analysis[31]

At the educational level, the work with a single subject N=1 can be very useful to develop the research by adopting experimental designs in order to arrive at evaluations of the effects of the implemented interventions that are as objective and replicable as possible, thus avoiding an evaluation based only on the descriptive observation of the learning phenomena. To have a system of programming, collection of the data and analysis of the data for the evaluation of the organized intervention, can facilitate the task of all the protagonists of the qualified intervention, balancing the need to maintain high standards of service and sustainability in workplaces with limited resources.

"*The methodology for planning and performing such kind of research focuses on examining the behavior of a single individual as time passes, monitoring the changes that occur following the introduction of particular types of intervention, which represent the independent variables of the experimental design as a fact*". (Cottini 2003)[32].

---

[31] The visual analysis of the data has made possible to verify the significance of the proposed educational intervention immediately. "*It is important that the data are placed on the graph to show the evolution of the behavior during the different stages of the experimental experience*", page 52, Lucio Cottini "*Fare ricerca con singoli soggetti*", 2016, IRFID.

[32] Cottini L., *"Fare ricerca con i singoli soggetti" Principi metodologici e applicazioni in educazione speciale e in psicologia clinica.* Page 7, IRFID, 2016.

Figure 3 - Graph "To stay at least 1 m away from the playmate"[33]

(Dates DD/MM/YY)

[33]The author thanks her colleague, Prof. Rosario Prencipe, for the technical support relating to the graphs showed in the book.

Figure 4 - Graph "Rate of the data of the eye contact with the playmate"

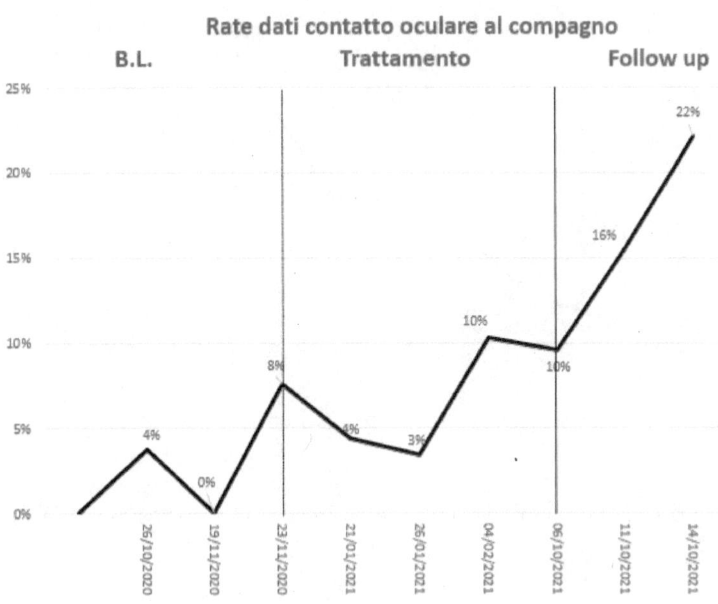

(Dates DD/MM/YY)

Figure 5 - Graph "Imitation"

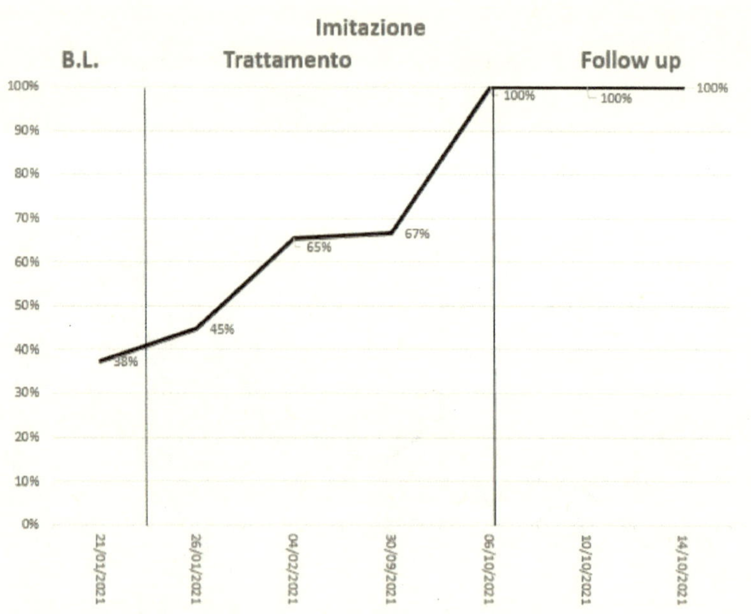

(Dates DD/MM/YY)

Discussion and conclusion

There has been the improvement of the target behaviors during the interaction in the gym through the Peteca game.

The main contribution of this work lies in having investigated the possibility of facilitating, through the use of methodological behavioral strategies (the Applied Behavior Analysis (ABA), which has its roots in the theories on the control and on the prediction of the conditions that contribute to describe the human behavior), the practice of sport for pupils with autism spectrum disorder, with the aim of supporting the school in finding valid strategies to avoid the discomfort of the pupils, who encounter obstacles in the acquisition of one or more skills constantly, and remain on the fringe of the social life, not just the school one, consequently.

This analysis reveals that the pervasive lack of a social response could be manipulated within a single-subject experimental design AB and would decrease, predictably, when the same pupils were encouraged to start appropriate preferred activities with students of their age. In addition, these procedures could be used to teach how to start preferred activities in public environments, with following reductions in the responses of escape and avoidance, also after the suggestions of the teacher have been removed completely, thus affecting the development of useful skills during the period of attendance at the compulsory school, such as, for example, to interact with the other pupils to perform a task, also a motor one, competently.

The activity designed and organized by me has allowed to raise the motivational component of the pupil, who paid attention to and interacted with several social partners, has reduced the unwanted behaviors (such as moving away from the classmates, not looking at them, etc.), and, at the same time, it increased his technical competence, perceiving himself effective both in the imitative task and in the proposed game.

The pupil, inserted in a small group of peers (classmates) with very different skills among them, experienced the fun in practicing the game and remained engaged, because he was able to find this experience as a positive one and he selected among the classmates that one, with whom he was able to create a good quality of social relationship. There is no doubt about the fact that the lack in the abilities and behavior of the children suffering from the autism spectrum disorder is a cause of social avoidance. Some scholars identify it as a strategy used to terminate the interactions, which are not reinforcing (reciprocally). If it is this way, it would not be surprising if the reverse were also true, that is, if a child can engage in preferred activities and, thus, can experience the success, the positive reinforcement would be achieved and the early stages of the treatment program could be more effective, if they were designed to maximize the chances of success of the same child. The illustration of this operational path lends itself to allowing a further methodological investigation and a reflection on our own daily work. This new way of research could incorporate the third wave of applied behavior analysis and be much more inclusive in terms of sport game at all levels.

Acknowledgements

To Dr. Rosaria Benincasa, whose precious teachings have opened up new ways of teaching, improving my work, and for having offered her enthusiastic and professional guidance for the realization of the book during the past year.

My personal and affectionate gratitude to the School Manager of the I.C. Di Giacomo 3 S. Chiara of Qualiano (Naples, Italy), Prof. Angela Carandente Sicca, with whom the collaboration has always been pleasant, and for having shown far-sightedness in starting this necessary experimentation, which is interesting for and involves the whole educational community.

To the colleagues for the availability shown towards the project, in particular to prof. Rosario Prencipe, to the pupils, Umberto, Cristian, Vincenzo, and Eduardo for their passionate and amused involvement in the proposed activities, and to their parents for their collaboration in spite of the difficulties in times of pandemic.

No less important is my partner Vincenzo, for all the hours spent viewing, cutting, and assembling the videos for the data collection, and for his involvement in this book, of which he is the author of the graphic design.

I hope that he feels it a little his too!

"Inequalities are the restraint of any social perspective of growth."

President of the Italian Republic, 2022, Sergio Mattarella

References

Baer, D M., Wolf, M.M. & Risley, T.R. (1987), "Some still current dimensions of applied behavior analysis", Journal of Applied Behavior Analysis.

Benincasa Rosaria BCBA® (2020), slides from the course "ABA e abilità accademiche Strategie di insegnamento dal curriculum base a quello intermedio", Sophis Academy.

Benincasa Rosaria BCBA® (2021), Slides "La Comunicazione aumentativa Alternativa", Sophis Academy online course.

Carroll, R.A., Joachim, B.T., St. Peter, C.C., & Robinson, N. (2015), "A comparison of error-correction procedures on skill acquisition during discrete trial training", Journal of Applied Behavior Analysis.

Carron, V.A., Colman.M. Michelle, Wheeler, "Cohesion and Performance in sport: A Meta Analysis", Journal of Sport and exercise Psychology, 2002, University of Western Ontario.

Cassamassima F., Traversetti M., "Programmazione per competenze - Dal Profilo di Funzionamento al PEI" (a cura di) Cajola Chiappetta L. Istituto Didattico, Settembre 2019.

Chevallier, C., Kohls, G., Troiani, V., Brodkin, E. S., & Schultz, R. T. (2012), "The social motivation theory of autism. Trends in cognitive sciences", 16 (4), 231-239.

Chevallier, C., Parish-Morris, J., McVey, A., Rump, K. M., Sasson, N. J., Herrington, J. D., & Schultz, R. T. (2015). "Measuring social attention and motivation in autism spectrum disorder using eye-tracking: Stimulus type matters. Autism Research", 8 (5), 620-628.

Chiappetta Cajola L. Rizzo A.L., Traversetti M., Bocci F., "I disturbi dello spettro dell'autismo: dagli esiti della formazione degli insegnanti alle politiche per l'inclusione", in Training actions and evaluation processes, Atti del Convegno internazionale SIRD.

Cooper J.O., Heron, T.E. & Heward, W.L (1997), "Applied Behavior Analysis". New York: MacMillan.

Cottini. L. (2016), "Fare ricerca con soggetti singoli", Nola: IRFID SRL.

Ermioni Katartzi E, Tzetzis G., Theodorakis M., P. Vlachopoulos S., Japanese Journal of Adapted Sport Science (2007), "Effects of goal setting and self-efficacy on Wheelchair basketball performance".

Fields, Patrice M. (2020). MSU Graduate Theses, "A Literature Review: Applied Behavior Analysis and Performance; the Past, the Present, and the Future", Missouri State University.

Grow, L.L. Carr, J.E., Kodak, T.M., Jostad, C.M., & Kisamore, A.N. (2011), "A comparison of methods for teaching receptive labeling to children with autism spectrum disorders", Journal of Applied Behavior Analysis.

Guazzo G.M. (2011), "L'analisi comportamentale applicata. Strategie educative per genitori e insegnanti", Nola, IRFID.

Iwata, B.A. (1997), "Negative reinforcement in applied behavior analysis: an emerging technology", Journal of Applied behavior analysis.

J. Johnston, H. Pennypacker (1993), "Strategies and tactics for human behavior research".

Katarina Rotta & Anita Li & Alan Poling, "Participants in Behavior-Analytic Sports Studies: Can Anybody Play Behavior Analysis in Practice".

Kazdin, A.E. & Bootzin, R.R. (1972), "The token economy: an evaluative review", Journal of Applied Behavior Analysis.

Koegel.L.R., University of California, Santa Barbara, Dyer., K The May Institute, Bell., L.K. University of California "The

Influence of child - preferred activities on Autistic children's Social Behavior".

Lovaas, O. I, (1982, August), "An overall evaluation of the young autism project", Paper presented to the American Psychological Association, Washington, DC.

MacDuff, G.S., Krantz, P.J. & McClannhan, L.E. (2001), "Prompts and prompt-fading strategies for people with autism. In C. Maurice, G. Green, & R.M. Fox (Eds.), Making a difference (pages 37-50)", Austin, TX: Pro-Ed.

Martin, J. J. (2006), "Psychosocial aspects of youth disability sport", Adapted Physical Activity Quarterly Wayne State University.

Martin, G. & Pear, J (2000), "Strategie e tecniche per il cambiamento. La via comportamentale", Milano McGraw-Hill.

McGhan, A.C., & Lerman, D.C. (2013), "An assessment of error-correction procedures for learners with autism", Journal of Applied Behavior Analysis, 46, 626-639.

Michael, J.L. (1993), "Concepts and principles of behavior analysis", Kalamazoo, MI: Society for the Advancement of Behavior Analysis.

Michael, J.L. (1993), "Concepts and Principles of Behavior Analysis. Revised Edition" Kalmazoo, MI: Association for Behavior analysis International.

Moderato P., Mancada Manforte, E. (1997), "Metodologia della ricerca in psicologia: pianificazione, controllo e misura". in P. Moderato, F. Rovetto (Eds) Psicologo: verso la professione, Milano McGraw-Hill.

Mulick, J.A. (1990), "The ideology and science of punishment in mental retardation", American journal of Mental Retardation.

Quaderni di Sport (2018), "Guida didattica per tutor e docenti della scuola primaria", Scuola dello Sport CONI, Calzetti & Mariucci Editori.

Ricci C., (2008), "ABA: Applied Behavior Analysis in D. Ianes and A. Canevaro (a cura di) L'integrazione scolastica", Trento Erickson.

Ricci C. (2005), "Valorizzare le differenze individuali", Trento Erikson.

Ricci C. (2012a), "La convenzione ONU sui diritti delle persone con disabilità: Lo scenario europeo nelle esperienze di applicazione dell'ICF in contesti socio-lavorativi. in O. Osio e P. Braibanti (a cura di)", Il diritto ai diritti, Milano Franco Angeli.

Richman D.M., Wacker D.P., Asmus J.M., and Casey S.D. (1998), "Functional analysis and extinction of different behavior problems exhibited by the same individual", Journal of Applied Behavior Analysis.

Romeo A. and Bellifemine D. (2013), "Trattamento delle stereotipie vocali attraverso una procedura di rinforzo differenziale dei comportamenti diversi e costo della risposta nel contest scolastico", "Disabilità Gravi".

Schultz, R. T. (2015), "Measuring social attention and motivation in autism spectrum disorder using eye-tracking: Stimulus type matters", Autism Research, 8 (5), 620-628.

Skinner B.F. (1957), "Verbal Behavior", Englewood Cliffs, NJ; Prentice - Hall.

Skinner B.F. (1953), "Science and human behavior", New York, MacMillan.

Skinner B.F. (1969), "Contingencies of reinforcement: A theoretical analysis", New York, Appleton Century Crofts.

Sundberg M.L. (2008), "Verbal behavior milestones assessment and placement program: The VB-MAPP", Concord, CA, AVB Press.

Sundberg M.L and Michael J (2001), "The benefit of Skinner's analysis of verbal behavior for children with autism", "Behavior Modification".

Sundberg M.L. and Partington J.W (1998), "The need for both discrete trial and natural environment language training for children with autism. In P.M. Ghezzi, W.L, Williams and J.E. Carr (a cura di)", Autism: Behavior analytic perspective, Reno, N.V, Context Press.

www.ingramcontent.com/pod-product-compliance
Lightning Source LLC
LaVergne TN
LVHW090127160826
845673LV00015B/1096

* 9 7 9 8 8 4 3 9 9 2 7 0 5 *